T0146675

BEHIND THE EYES

BEHOLD, THE DREAMER COMETH

AUHMEIN GREEN

authorHOUSE®

AuthorHouse™
1663 Liberty Drive
Bloomington, IN 47403
www.authorhouse.com
Phone: 1 (800) 839-8640

© 2018 Auhmein Green. All rights reserved.

No part of this book may be reproduced, stored in a retrieval system, or transmitted by any means without the written permission of the author.

Published by AuthorHouse 05/11/2018

ISBN: 978-1-5462-4216-1 (sc)
ISBN: 978-1-5462-4215-4 (e)

Print information available on the last page.

Any people depicted in stock imagery provided by Getty Images are models, and such images are being used for illustrative purposes only. Certain stock imagery © Getty Images.

This book is printed on acid-free paper.

Because of the dynamic nature of the Internet, any web addresses or links contained in this book may have changed since publication and may no longer be valid. The views expressed in this work are solely those of the author and do not necessarily reflect the views of the publisher, and the publisher hereby disclaims any responsibility for them.

New International Version (NIV)
Holy Bible, New International Version®, NIV® Copyright ©1973, 1978, 1984, 2011 by Biblica, Inc.® Used by permission. All rights reserved worldwide.

INTRO

In the body of Christ there are many who carry many giftings. There are some who possess the gift of healing, wisdom, interpretation, exhortation, prophecy etc. Overtime, I've discovered the giftings that I possess. Which leads me to my first point; Throughout the bible it shows in certain events, or ways of how God reveal things, or in ways he speaks. So, I would like to focus on the ability of a dreamer, and the things that are foreseen. As an individual who has discovered two types of people; people who are visionaries and dreamers. However, there are those who carry both gifting's. Dreamers are people who see dreams while asleep and entering further into deeper realms of dreams; On the contrary, the gift of the visionaries occurs while awake. But dreams and visions go much further than just seeing, but it takes understanding of what an individual is seeing. Which leads me to my focus; One of the gifts that I possess is being a dreamer. Being able to see things beforehand, things that are beyond this world, that the natural mind can't articulate at times. Many people, even in ancient history, dreamers have not been accepted, or should I say rejected. As a result, some individuals don't believe in dreamers. Some individuals just believe it's just a fantasy. From the years of my youth I've dream so much.

I've seen things that I couldn't interpret or put into words of what I've seen. At times it seems so real, and even felt real. I could feel so many emotions. It seems the more depth I went in dreams it became reality. My dreams started manifesting into reality. Being young I didn't understand this gift, or how to understand it. There was moment I would share and seem that I was receptive but rejected. So, I would suppress what I'd seen. It seems that they weren't listening to me at times. It was like they heard me but didn't hear me. I began to grow not only in age but spiritually. I started maturing in my gift, trying to understand who I was. After a while, I began questioning God. I started asking him to reveal to me my giftings. Eventually, I began seeing these gifts that I operated in. Can you imagine feeling every bit of emotion, or seeing things beyond your norm? What about seeing those you love getting hurt, or death? I began to write this book around the age of 17 yrs. old. But before I started writing I was prophesied that my dreams will become a book, so I was told to start writing them down; and that's when I began. For a moment, I would like to reach out to those who are biblical readers. There is biblical evidence that God spoke through dreams, revealing himself, or his mysteries etc. There have being symbolic things shown in dreams. Individuals can't even imagine the capacity that God has revealed and can reveal. God is mysterious, and he works in mysterious ways. Another discovery, is that I've happen to understand and realize that dreamers obtain the eyes of a seer and they are one. My dreams have been prophetic, supernatural, and forewarning; I've foreseen things before it happened. And God have also shown me people and their circumstances.

But eventually, the dreams manifest days later, or a day after, a week, or a month or years from now. Don't take what you see lightly, you can happen to be the key to change someone's life, or an attacker blocker, or even a destiny changer. Even through the rejections, never stop seeing or accepting who or what you are.

DREAM

It was me and some other individuals in this house and my cousin had food. There was a snake, slithering, and it spit on his food. It passes everyone else and it heads towards me. I was in front of the door, jumping on the chair, and the snake jump and attack me. In response, I screamed in fear, shaking it off me. Particularly, in this dream I didn't know what it was, but it had frightened me. So, I didn't understand why it would pass the others and coming directly to me.

But time after time I would dream certain things but could never remember the entire dream, except certain parts.

In ancient time, people of the old would express a saying that to dream of snakes you have an enemy, or enemies. Also, there was another wise saying, "when dreaming of snakes kill it." But because of fear, I was too afraid to face or kill what was detrimental to me. I've understood over the years that fear has a way to keep an individual limited, or restricted. It keeps a person from living the way they should, or prevailing. But when face with what I feared most I would usually run from it instead of facing it. Sometimes we as people we run too much, and as we continued to run we never know how to face our issues. We run from problems which sometimes occur in wrong timing.

DREAM

I was at my aunt house, and my cousin had a box of snakes and he allowed them to scatter. So, I went home and went to sleep, and I woke up the next morning, recognizing that there was a snake blending with the plug, and I hollered, and it slither away.

We sometimes are afraid to face what we need to face. As well there are vessels of the enemy, and those individuals have agendas to sabotage. There main agenda is to keep what's within restricted. So, the enemy utilizes people, or the things in your environment to become opposition, or create hostility. Which leads to God forewarning and exposing agendas or the heart. I'm reminded of Joseph in the bible who carried the gift of the dreamer. Joseph foreseen many things concerning his future, and through being a spokesman of what he saw; he talked in a hostility environment. Being disliked and rejected of what he seen will transpire. Joseph brothers plotted against him, they despised him. There jealous became hatred, and their hatred turned into a horrible act. Later, as a fulfillment of the dream Joseph was place in the palace; he later faces those same people who oppress him and sold him. This shows how family can be intimidated and try destroying. So, they shoot words of hostility; trying to oppress, or bring distress (Genesis 37).

Joseph not only had the gift of the dreamer, but the gift of interpretation.

Another example, Judas was at the table with Jesus and the disciples. Jesus and the disciples were having the last supper. While committing their body and mind to the sacred moment, Judas was plotting Jesus betrayal. The time came of betrayal and Judas kiss him and the army of men captured Jesus. But Jesus knew the truth, he knew who was for him and against him; but Judas regrets it.

DREAM

I was at this person's house and there were a lot of people. Everybody left except for two people. We sat down on the ground, and we see a snake, and everyone jumps up. But the ironic things were the snake was more focus on me. So, it was coming towards me. I tried smothering it with the pillow, but it was coming too fast and I woke up.

I am a witness to being called and chosen and the weight that comes with being chosen. It seems there's a bounty, an assigned assassin who must make it their job to demolish. The adversary has been known to steal, kill, and destroy. At a young age I was seeing things that I had no idea what I was seeing or what it meant. Around the age of 4yrs old or up; one night I was lying in the chair behind my aunt and it was dark. I remember leaning over her, seeing a white snake slithering on the floor.

I woke her up, "Aunt Leslie do you see that snake?"

She spoke, "no boy, now go to sleep."

But I couldn't go back to sleep. I was disturbed to be the only one to have seen it. I never understood it. Being young and understanding that I was different and that I wasn't the usual kid. What was spoken before my time of existences is very much validated and approved. I can't erase even if tried. I tried so many times to get away from it, running. But I seem to find myself in another unusual moment; the same snake I saw in the living room I saw it again in a different room. I was afraid to get off the bed. Being surrounded by darkness you become afraid to move forward, or to even make any movements. Fear creates stagnation, and a sense of numbness. The enemy will make you seem afraid to conquer your fears or accept the fact you're who God created you to be. Being chosen there's so much required of us, and the enemy comes to devoured those that know nothing about themselves. He targets individuals who have identity crisis, people who are trying to understand who they are and whose they are. When you don't understand your future, or your destiny you are lost in whom you are.

There are many spiritual interactions that occurs in the heavens (atmosphere). Which lead me to the approach of expounding of demons, demonic operations, angels. Throughout history you've heard of witches, warlocks, angels etc. So, I would to express that demons are real and there are things that happens beyond the natural seeing eye.

DREAM

I was at this church and I left. I and my mom were following these people, but they didn't want us to follow them. I remembered we were flying in the air and I could see demons in the atmosphere. As we were high up, one was trying to grab me, but I went beneath it. They were trying to detour me. So, we kept following the people until we got to the place that was familiar. We got there, and I saw this house and this person I knew.

I woke up and went in the spirit, praising God. Immediately, I enter in my heavenly language and God begin to speak; telling me that I'm wanted by the enemy. The devil wanted me, and he wants me to dead. For those that know nothing about yourself or your purpose, ask God. There's a lot more to the ordinary and what you see in your daily life. Don't take what is tangible to the eyes, ears, or any other senses lately. It's something deeper, beyond the eyes, beyond the earthly realm. Understand your gifts, because there are giftings that we as people obtain and yet not knowing our identity. The enemy sees our potential that is why the attacks are so intense. There are times when we try to warn people that something is about to happen, or you tell them the things you were seeing. They yet not believe it. It seems that they give the deaf ear and they don't listen. There were times I've seen things in my dreams and it happened. God will allow you to be steps ahead of your opponent, or ahead of time. It's up to us to know what it is and be receptive of it. There were situations that I was entangled in and I would dream of the very event and what would happen. I would see it and the next day it happened I failed the test. I was weakened to my struggles and my secrecy. I can admit there were many temptations that I faced, and before they ever occurred I dreamed and the moment after I was fatal to it. Time after time It kept coming back until I was able to conquer and defeat it.

DREAM

I was with people and we were holding a bucket of snakes and one got out. The color of the snake was yellow and white it turned around and look at me. It begins to move so fast, approaching me. I was told not to move. No one else was approached. I've come to realization that the enemy can come in your very presence and will not even touch you.

DREAM

I was in this house and this person was pouring oil on the floor. And I remember me having this little boy with me. I went outside, and this snake came up trying to strike me, but I jump over it. There were a bunch of snakes on the ground pile up.

I woke up. After the dreamed I told my leader about it. she begins to give me words.

Years of stories, I heard from my mom and other relatives that in my youth age I use to go in deep trance, crying, and they couldn't wake me up. They didn't understand what was going on. They explained to me how I would speak in tongues and going around laying hands. It was described that while in the womb I would move around extremely, flowing across her belly. As a result, she would enter the ground of the church and it triggers a major response. In fear, she read the bible continuously, stayed in church. The songs she sung carried such weight that in her pregnancy term it produces such a tremendous interaction. She explained to me how her and my dad would read the bible to me.

DREAM

It was dark, and I could barely see. And I began falling off these steps-like cliffs. As I was falling, I literally ended up rolling off the bed and I awoke.

In dreams I would run for my life because the opponent was trying to kill me. I fought for my life day and night. There was this one time I seen in a dream something happened to my mom. At times my dream is so critical that it feels real to me. The emotions that I feel I would wake up feeling what I felt. There were moments I seen my mother death, and it frightened me.

One morning I was sleep I remember my grandma praying. And I was dreaming, and I end up getting stuck.

DREAM

Me and some other people were running. There were people who was in a helicopter and they jumped out after us. Some were close, but we kept running. We came upon this neighborhood. I wanted to go home but I couldn't wake up. So, I pinch myself and I didn't feel anything. The only time I was able to awaked was when my grandma called my name. Immediately when she calls my name I awoke.

There were dreams that would contain demons that seem to be bigger than I. They chase me, and I ran for my life. Mankind and scientists have certain theories, statements that have doubted what has been seen was created from something that has been eaten, or some late-night horror movie. There are people who reject dreamers, doubt them, restrict them etc. In the beginning of the discovery of my Christian journey, there was a point in my life where I had no clue who I was, or the giftings within me. I remember sitting in church on the front row and this prophet who was a member of the church, stood up, and begin to prophesy. She spoke what God told her to say to me and it was that I was a prophet. From that day on it was confirm through different men and women of God. But one Friday night service an evangelist by the name of Joyce Allen, and a pastor by the name Otis Allen. Pastor Otis was playing his keyboard and I was in the spirit with my eyes close. Suddenly, he came to me, swooping me off my feet, and begins to prophesy. He spoke plain and clearly about me stop running from who I was chosen to be. That very moment changed the course of my life. Publicly proclaiming what God has spoken to him to say. After that moment, I went to go to God for myself and sought him for answers; and he started revealing unto me certain gifts.

DREAM

I was in this car and my sister opens the door trying to pull me out, while the vehicle was moving. I was fighting her off me. Then she would disappear and then out of nowhere she appeared to the other side car and tried to pull me out.

DREAM

My God Mom was showing me her pastor new church and I begin to ask her about the old church and she showed me where it was. We began to walk through the woods and as we were walking wolves were behind us. Eventually, they went their way, and my God sister started to run. Immediately, the wolves turned around chasing us. My God mom fell, and she disappear. I pick up a stick fighting them off, hiding behind this tree and as I was hiding more wolves were coming I swung hitting them as they were coming. Eventually, I ran from behind the tree, and seeing these people and trying to reach them. But the wolves were striking at me. As I got closer a snake was wrapped around this person, striking at me. One snake attempted to attack me, but I was holding on to it and it miss and I tried to cut it.

When getting closer to destiny there are challenges. However, there seem to be battles before reaching the people you must reach, or your designated destination. After seeing the dream, it startles me, causing me to awake. Immediately, waking up speaking in tongues. Demons are real, and they are a systematically organized. They are release in the earth realm, into earthen vessels that are weak minded, vulnerable, and not as strong. They have agendas to assassinate or bring restriction to what lies within. As you get closer to your purpose and get higher in God the more; the devil will try everything in his power to stop you from getting to the place where you need to be.

DREAM

There were people after me. So, I ran to house and I lock the door. Me, thinking that I'm safe; the person starts kicking at the door as he was kicking it, the lock was unlocking. So, I tried to rush to the door before it came unlock fully. As soon as I got to it he kicked it open. I was in this place where people were trying to kill me I was running trying to get to a place. I believe there were people chasing me and the other people.

DREAM (JUNE 2014)

I dreamed of a demon, and a friend of mine was the demon. And I was speaking in tongues.

Speaking in unknown tongues is one of many gifts. It is one of the evidence of having the Holy Spirit. When entering unknown tongues, the spirit makes intercession. It becomes an open communication between heaven and the spirit. So, when words cannot be articulated, the spirit speaks (Rom. 8:26). There's more to just having that gift; it strengthens you personally. It helps edify, to show the unbelievers that God is real (1 Cor. 14:22).

We have certain people who are connected to us and we think that they have the best interest for us. If you're not wise enough or don't have discernment you wouldn't know their agendas. Some people don't want to see growth and prosperous life. You have dream killers, birthright killers and those who don't want to see you be happy. In the bible, King Herod was after Jesus from birth to kill him. But King Herod had sent others to seek his location. King Herod tried stopping destiny (Matthew 2 (NIV)). The question is can you identify your opponent? Or are you your own dream killer? Birthright killer? What God has already predestined from the beginning of time I don't care how many witches, warlocks, demons, and serpents are after you. They can't stop what's already planned. It's already written who you are meant to be. We each have a role to fulfilled, but it's up to you to understand who you are. We all have a choice.

DREAM

A person was chasing me and another individual. I went down these stairs trying to get away from him. Every time I would see an escape I would take it to get away.

DREAM (JUNE 5TH)

A person was chasing me, and I ended up grabbing him and snapping his neck. But he got up and told me that I was going to die. He was persistent to come after me. We got away and got in different cars to get away from them, so they couldn't catch us. But we ended up getting kidnapped. They took us to this place and in this place was sinful. They held us hostage. I've seen people dead. However, every chance I had I would try to escape, but someone would get me. I had almost escape. But I saw someone coming so I ran back inside. The woman that tried to help had set me up. She was smiling. Finally, I had got away and was able to run. While running I saw these houses, saw the person who was chasing us, so we hid; but they saw us.

Then I started to run to another place but behind me was the person with a gun. Sooner than later we got away. I thought that I would never escape or get away. I was wondering how long we would be here.

While seeing this dream, I was in a predicament that seemed that it would've never end. Every time I tried doing what God chosen me to do there was a great struggle. I would be tempted with a great amount of temptation. While being in that battle, mentally it was destroying me, breaking me down; seem like I was about to lose it. Being that I was weak to the temptation, I failed. It was like every time I failed, it would come back again. Before it would come I could foresee the situation. There were times where I resisted the enemy from any sexual interaction. It seems as if it was a hindrance; which it was. Every time I got closer, closer, and closer to God I had to fight even harder. The warfare became intense. It was like something would pull me down to point where I couldn't function. There's time where it seems as if I was going to lose my mind. We have heard the familiar saying why me? I had even asked that question to God, why me? At one point I threw in the towel in my life, because of the pressure I was under. It seems even in throwing in the towel it didn't make it better. So, I went back to pick up that same towel I threw down. Sometimes the struggles we fight internally can be overbearing. It seemed like we will never escape from bondage, or from being a failure. The situation gets worse and worse. However, there are times where we see there's no escaping. Different situations create a variety emotion. It causes some to feel unqualified, depress, oppress, and unworthy. If not careful and knowing how to handle the emotions, it'll began to affect the process of the dream; which turns into reality. We start to think that we will never be who we are meant to be, or we will never fulfill our biggest dreams. So, we run and run from who we are because we have no faith in ourselves. Our minds become cloudy which creates weariness. And we stop believing, and we go into a stage of death. Which causes the dreamer to become weary in sight, not seeing clearly, or acceptance of what's foreseen.

DREAM

I was casting out demons out of these two women. And their spirits had switched. One demon came out of one lady; but the other one was hard. I remember calling out the name of the demon. There were two names, but I could only remember one. I called out the spirit of a liar. On the contrary, I remember riding with this other person. But I was driving somewhere. Afterwards, I was backing out and collided into another car; and I had to tell the person who was driving that car. Also, I call my grandma. She came, and she told us to walk.

DREAM

I was in this church and I remember these people wanted me to go with them somewhere. At first, I was going to go, but I had changed my mind. However, me and another individual was in this place. And I remember seeing this

15

gun in front of this person. I picked it up, and I became stuck while the person was trying to kill me. My life was in critical danger. The person who had the gun was holding me hostage, preventing me from going home. Finally, I escaped by running home. As I was running towards home, there was another person who was running and ran ahead of me.

DREAM (OCTOBER 14, 2014)

There was an event going on. And there were these people who came. A lady I know was sitting at the table with her head down; looking as if she was going to cry. Pastor told me to give her a hug. Eventually, I did. As I was hugging the lady, I started to speak in tongues. Consequently, there was this prophet and I touched her back. However, she had something to tell our Pastor.

When you understand the significance of reaching the people who need you and waits for your arrival. Obstacles and restrictions won't be what interfering with who, or what you have reach.

DREAM

I was in my house and there was a snake on the floor as if it was dead. My mom was trying to kill it, but she was afraid. The snake wasn't moving so she finally picks it up and brings it to my face knowing I feared it. So, I react. I became scared and started to panic. Suddenly, there was a movement and the snake got away quick. It escaped through the crack of my front door. I told someone to look and see if it was there and they open it, but it wasn't there.

Question, when it's time to come face to face with your issues or your enemies are you ready?

DREAM

I was at this place and this person I know was telling me that I was related to this individual since I was young. She gave me a piece of paper with words that she wanted me to say to the person. Repeating what was wrote, I repeat the words. My sister had done something to me and I hit her. In response, my mom said that she was going to call the police. I said, "So, call them." I packed my stuff and they told me that I was going to be in jail for 30 days.

DREAM

I was inside this house. But I wasn't the only person inside. I open the front door, leaving, and I saw this snake. So, I came back inside. Then there was this person that had something in his hands. However, opening the door, and in came the snake. I ran on the bed and close the door. But one night it seems like at nights things would come out or happen. I woke up and look on the walls there were big black spiders; and on the floor was the snake. This person was about to get off the bed and I said that there was a snake on the floor. Ironically, the snake turned into a human boy. I didn't have any oil, so

I anointed myself. The boy told me that he'll be back and bring a love sacrifice.

There are moments my dreams can be very horrifying, and some wouldn't believe in the things I see. Some wouldn't be able to handle it. Dreams can be very realistic, but many undermine them. Many times, dreamers are misunderstood.

DREAM (SEPTEMBER 14ᵀᴴ)

Me and other individuals were talking to this demon, if not mistaken. I was outside of this place and seen this not normal thing. It was white and wearing all black. He began moving closer to me. Dimen puts a knife to Montavius ear. So, I ask her why she was doing what she was doing. Through the harassing all he did was laugh. He went home, and I went running after him. As I was running I begin to levitate in the air and was able to touch the tree outside of my home. My Godmother and mother pulled up. Then the setting changed. AJ burned his arm and his shorts caught on fire; his pants were flammable. However, I and Tammy started to walk, and I saw this trap. It was a hammer hanging down tide to something. My aunt ran in and nothing happened. But me running in triggered the trap. Then I finally got free of the net. It was a struggle for a while. It was revealed of the person that set the trap for me. So, I became mad. After, I saw my dad crying and needed comfort.

After the dream, later, there was a trap. But it wasn't for me. It was for a close relative of mine (grandmother) and the person she was dealing with was involved. One of the preachers of the church had drop me off home that night and got caught into the cross fire. They had surrounded him, while he was in his car.......

In different dreams there are symbolism and interpretation; like colors, clothing, and animals etc. The question is, how to identify and understanding the very small details, or the things that stand out.

DREAM

There was this Apostle by the name of Apostle Mars. I heard that this Apostle was in the hospital. I went to go see her and as I was coming I saw her son and them leaving, and her daughter. I got back, and she was with the drug addicts, homeless, people that needed help. She was wearing her purple and black robe. There was this woman who did not like me for some reason, and I didn't even know why. The woman was talking junk to me. Apostle Mars was walking up the street and there were people behind following her.

Sometimes in dreams there are deeper revelation and greater depth of sight. Example, Joseph was interpreting two men who were imprisoned who had dreams. They explained everything that was seen in the dream. Due to him having the gift of interpretation, he seen details, and explain what everything meant. Also, how it would occur exactly (Genesis 40). Behind the eyes of dreamers there are much prolific insight. On the contrary, sometimes there are times when dreams will transition from one place to another. Like in the beginning of the book noticed how some of the dreams setting changes.

DREAM

There was an eagle that landed on people draining them. As well capable of taking away their power through its nails but I ran before he could get to me. There was more to it, but I can't remember it.

DREAM

There were three thrones in the sky and sitting upon the thrones were three beings, but you could hardly see them. My mother and the other parents took their kids to see them. All the kids were in a line. But the man that was sitting on the throne said, "you all have been disobedient".

Due to the response, I became upset, and I began to wonder why us? What about our parents? So, I walked to this house to get somebody and the voice told me to come back I told him I'm going to get somebody. I got there, getting people. I sat in the car being nonresponsive, due to being upset. My mother said something to me, and afterwards we went to this house and waited for someone. I recall us walking down the side of the road. And I was walking behind this woman and other people. While walking, there was a woman who pushed me; and I had this look. So, she apologizes but I spoke in tongues. However, the woman was label to be a prophet. She embraces me, telling me something, and we both fall to the ground. As we examine this dream and understanding the significance of thrones. Thrones represent seat of power and authority. Not only just that but noticed there were three beings; and biblical the number three represent the trinity: the father, son, and holy spirit. When dreaming be attentive of the small details.

DREAM (SEPTEMBER 29TH)

I was in water, not only was it just me but I seen this girl in the water. The ironic thing is she had no idea how to swim. Somehow someone taught her how. But someway and somehow, I began to drown. I couldn't move, and I couldn't even get up if I tried. Furthermore, noticing the house flooded. Therefore, I began to float, stuck, as the water moved me under the chair. No one noticed me drowning.

DREAM (APRIL 3, 2013)

There was a lot of water that was overflowing around my bed and outside. I was able to speak to it, commanding it to leave. Afterwards, I seen two people who had moved into new houses; which were my mother and Elder Shay.

Nevertheless, water have a variety of meanings. One representation is it can represent the troublesome times in life. It can represent a cleansing or can represent the enemy; depending on meaning of what you're seeing.

Which leads me to another dream that show symbolism…

DREAM

An aunt of mine, who goes by the name of Nadine. She was told that she was a spiritual father and the man said, "you got to keep her in your prayers." But she said something about receiving fire. However, there was a prophet who name was Gaines. And he was praying for her and a person name Montavius. Later, it was something strange that happen. It started raining hail and, in the mix, I was praising God. Afterwards, I remember AJ running to me, being that I had forgot about him.

Do you noticed in the dream she was called a father? It sounds strange, doesn't it? Side bar, many times you mothers, or women who take the "role" of a man. Then you have those who try to be a man. But understand the importance of a man, "a father". A father is what gives structure to the family, not only does he give stability. But he's what keeping balance. So pretty much he's the foundation of the house and if there no foundation then there's not structure. The father gives structure, he's what keeps the house standing and a mother is what keeps the house together. The mother teaches, nurtures, loves while the father gives guidance, substances, strength etc. So, within the dream shows a prophecy going forth. Also, warning about that gives structure will need support. In all words she'll need prayer because of the role she has comes with a great weight. However, that wasn't the only symbolic symbol. Additionally, a spiritual father is a religious teacher or guide, esp. one instrumental in leading a soul to God. Father means "life giver".

DREAM (AUGUST 23ʀᴅ)

Me and my sisters were running from these people. As a result, we defended ourselves. I told them to use their abilities to get away. One of them can fly so she flew to the tree. And the other had speed, so she swiftly ran to the tree. Together we touch the tree and as we touch it a protection shield was lifted around us. But they kept coming closer and closer. So, we let go of the tree. Immediately, I touched this woman, looking at her, commanding her to die. After I touch her she went crazy. They were persistent in killing me. I was able to get away and hid. They couldn't find me, but I heard a man say, "he has great powers, we have to get him."

DREAM (NOVEMBER 26TH)

There were these people and these creatures which were gray, with funny looking mouths. They were in groups heading towards a ship. So, me and others follow from behind. We had to pay money to get on the ship and when we got on, we started moving. As we were moving we were about to go over a cliff. Because of that two-people jumped off, getting their money back. Then I jump off, giving me my money back. I was afraid. The scenery changes to a school setting. There was a girl who said something mean to me while walking by. In response, I kept walking, paying it no mind. Then I was in cafeteria seeing people I knew. But to distinguish, there was this dude I knew. He was sitting across from me and sitting beside a girl that I like. And I told him I liked her. He started smiling. Then there was a girl who said something to the other girl, commenting on her hair. The girl didn't like it, which led to everyone laughing. On the contrary I heard a student and teacher in confrontation. Afterwards, the scenery changes again. We were in a setting of a restaurant. This Apostle, who name was Mars she was cooking. Consequently, me, Mars, and my godmother went to the back to talk. And I explained how this person had said something to me and responded. I was then told how mean the comment was. Next, I got drop off home, going to help kids getting ready. Before I got out of the car, I explained to mars I had a prophetic dream to share with her.

DREAM (AUGUST 13, 2014)

I was a protector. First, protector of a baby. Then I went to another level and became a knight. I was clothed in armor, holding a sword and other weapons. Then I seen three eggs. I and some other individuals were in the water preparing to fight. But there was a big bird that lost her eggs and she was coming for them. In her coming we spread out, preparing. She came, and we began to throw her in the air, and the more we did, pieces of her came off.

DREAM (SEPTEMBER 20, 2014)

Two crowns.

In dreams God speaks to individuals allowing them to see what is happening in the present time, or upcoming future events. However, immaturity causes misunderstanding. So, it leaves the mind open to wondering what is been process through sight. Many times, what's been proceeded it becomes frightened and unbearable to handle. There are dreams where God will allow you to see yourself to bring correction where there's error, or to foresee things to come. Which leads to a misunderstanding because not being able to identify when God is speaking or giving direction. There's a lot of things that occurs within the dream realm. Don't become afraid of what you are hearing or seeing. That's the time where we as people should be getting closer to God. If you noticed when correction comes, we as people don't like it. We become angry with the words coming from the mouth of God. If you noticed in that dream the woman pushes me and I become angry. And afterwards she was apologetic. Being corrected and chastise don't feel good. Furthermore, true chastise comes with love and making a person better. The pushing process result in aggravation, becoming frustrated with the stretching. When there's a pulling there's a taring and irritableness. Apart of being a dreamer is being stretch beyond limitations and understanding the birthing that's happening within the dreamer. On the contrary, there are a variety of things dreamers face. First, but one of the major affliction is rejection. Secondly, mental warfare. Thirdly, identity crisis; not understanding the shaping of destiny, or where they fit at times. Therefore, dreamers have a very valuable gift. Because they have the ability of foresight. So, if the enemy can infect dreamers by getting into their minds, and their hearts. He can cripple their ability to see and understand.

On the other hand, sometimes dreams can backwards, the opposite. I have heard people say when you dream of a man it's a woman. I remember dreaming about this young girl that I knew, and she was with child. The dream showed me her having a boy with a head full of hair. In discovery, she had a beautiful little girl, naming her Skylar. But there were moments the people I seen were the exact individual. So, I beg a difference; the saying is somewhat true. What you don't understanding you seek and find answers. There are multiple ways in finding out dreams. Never dismiss what you see. There are times where what you see seem foolish.

1 cor 1: 27

"But God chose the foolish things of the world to shame the wise; God chose the weak things of the world to shame the strong."

What seem foolish, or worthless, have much in store. There are things that seem to not have value but are worth more in utilizing. So, understand that God can take what doesn't make sense, to make sense. Never degrade or demote what has potential but doesn't look useable.

DREAM

There was a fish that I had but looking within the tank there were many.

After seeing the dream, come to find out that one of my family members was pregnant. However, fish often seen as a symbol of fertility and personal growth. Also, research shows seeing fish swimming may symbolize conception. Which leads to the understanding of impregnation.

DREAM

I was at this place and war was going on. There were people who wouldn't let us leave. Suddenly, a golden, thick mist came over us.

The color gold often symbolizes what it does elsewhere: wealth, power, and status. At times it can mean endures and withstand fire. Don't take what you see lightly it could be a warning to let you know you're in danger or the people you see. Be careful and watchful of what's to come. As the world evolve, there are a lot that will begin to change. If you haven't noticed now, how the world has become more corrupted. Dreams have a way in teaching you how to be prepared and watchful of the signs. Many times, in certain regions, in the heavenly realms there are demonic activities that are occurring and have manifested in the earthen vessels. Be girded and prayerful. There are many areas that the enemy work in to start confusion, or corruption. Which can lead to a war. Understand the time.

DREAM

There was this very tall boy who picks my mother up and held her to the wall. I ran behind him and slam him to the ground. I thought he was down, but he wasn't. Then he ran behind me again and I had slid. Then the dream transition to this person I called my brother; his name is Paul. He and his mom had moved to a different location. But he wasn't too happy. Afterwards, my aunt was telling me that she called him. And he told her that he moved.

DREAM

Apostle Mars and her son had this big church. I had seen her and went over greeted them with a hug and handshake. Afterwards, people started to come in and the apostle put on her robe. However, the ironic thing was I didn't have on my glasses. So, my vision was blurry. I was in search of them.

During the time of these dreams I had about them I didn't really know them. They had come to the church that I was under at that time. That's when I had seen them for the first time. After that night I began to dream of meeting them. Finally, as time went by I met them, and I grew to know them.

DREAM (APRIL 11TH)

I was about to be late for school. My mom had drop me off to this neighborhood, so that I would hurry an

On the contrary, God show you people that are in need and need intercession. He awakes you in the midnight hours, getting your attention and taking the initiative to intercede.

DREAM

There was this young woman that went to the same church I went to. However, she was hurt about something an individual had done to her. Furthermore, this person I knew were about to do something sexual with another.

After the dream, I call my leader and told her this dream. I told her what I seen, and about the individual that was within the dream. My leader confirmed to me that the young lady has been hurt by a person that she was dealing with. It was so different for me; because I knew nothing of what she was encountering.

DREAM

I saw this person I knew, and he was reading the bible about homosexuality. But the ironic thing that happen was a bug coming from beneath the carpet.

In my discovery of understanding the dream. I find out that bugs represented demonic activities. And even during that time, I questioned. I told my mother about the dream, not really understanding. But in our discussion, she explained to me of what it could've been; and her very words were, "he could be dealing with it" But me being in my beginning Christianity walk, I was in disbelief. I didn't understand the deep things that leaders dealt with in secret. Overtime, the truth came was reveal. The secret that was hidden was no longer hidden. The individual came open enough to show identity. However, the individual hidden struggle became no longer a fight against self but more like a submission. Due to what I seen, I was reminded of the city of Sodom and Gomorrah. If you don't understand so far now, dreams are real. An example.... There was a married couple who was staying at a location. Before moving, I dreamed of them moving into a new house. Later, I called the wife and told her. Not only did I see her living in a new house, also saw her speaking in tongues; which was very unusual for her. As a result, month and days later they end up moving into a new place and I call and reminded her. I said, "you remember when I told you I had that dream that you had a new house?" she said "yeah". There are a lot times that I dream about people. It's like I'm able to see into their life, seeing the issues, opportunities, or attacks etc.

Years ago, I dreamed about my aunt and I could hear her speaking in tongues. Till this day it hasn't happen yet. I wait for her to fully get in the posture to be receptive of the spirit of God and his infilling in her life. My point of saying that is to show that there will be things foreseen and yet not manifested. I've seen it too many times for it not manifest. There are dreams that take time. So, years from now they may come into fruition.

THE YEAR OF 2013

This was the year I was discovering who I was. As I grew and sought God, things began to reveal. Also, another year where I was facing many obstacles.

DREAM (JANUARY 15TH)

There were two couples who were having problems.

A woman, by the name of Lynette, was standing at her seat. And these people were at the front of the altar. There was a woman up there and Lynette did what the lord had told her to do. I stood there and watch. Her son, Montavius, went up there, saying something to his mom. But he was out of order, so whatever he said was wrong. We left, and he did something that kind of upset me. And I chose to walk home. But his mom had felt someway of his actions. So, her mom was telling her she needed to talk to him. She felt as if he did it to get back at her.

THE YEAR OF 2014

DREAM (MARCH 7TH)

Some individual was chasing me and some other people. It was something that we had that he wanted. Then there was a scene where JH Rose was becoming taken over. There were no teachers, until there was a surrender. After they surrendered teachers started to come and it resume back to normal.

DREAM (JUNE 24TH)

My mom and some of my church family were in this place. And my mom was talking about how she didn't know how to love her first son. Then, a sister of church, by the name of Latoya Wiggins, started crying. But she said something about her mind. Afterwards, I seen my cousin praising God. As well, there was a mother of the church, by the name of Helen. She started to cry out, opening her mouth explaining how she had similar feelings. But I went into my heavenly language.

Identifying truth births deliverance. Not only your deliverance but others door to freedom. Understand what happens when your honest, not only with self but others.

DREAM (JULY 3RD)

I was in this place and I wanted to leave, but they didn't want me to leave. Finally, I was able to leave, and, in my escape, I ran. While I was running there were different doors and someone from behind chasing me. The individual was trying to restrain me, keeping me where I was. One door I was fighting the individual as he tried hindering me. I escape, coming to the last door. This last door had demons; I came out of the building running for my life. Then, I got to this other place, seeing old people praising the lord. There was a man who called me a doctor and another man out of nowhere came out a room. So, I ran again. This while running I ran into a wall full of televisions. But awkward thing, is that it warned me about a woman coming after me. There was another person who escape where they tried restraining me. And they were coming after the person. However, there was a man who had a remote, controlling people mind. The remote command them to do what he want them to. I snatched the it from him, stopping him, and used it on him. Scenery changes: we were at this other place. There were clothes, so we hid. But somehow, they caught up with us. So, they found the girl, taking her away. But I created a distraction by making noise. The woman stops, thinking and decided not to take her away.

Who you are is very much a threat to the enemy. So, he'll try to keep you, or what's in your limited. As well, try to manipulate the mind with certain things. You've heard me say throughout this entire book, there are individuals who need you. There's a future of people who are connect to you. So, you must live and fight.

DREAM (JULY)

A friend of mine was dating this girl, who was discussing about doing something. So, I whisper in his ear, telling him not to. She was proclaiming to be pregnant and I was explaining to him that it wasn't his because she was with someone else. Then there was a moment where I seen a huge hand coming through the window and snatched down what seem to look like curtains. (This dream came from when I was in a toxic friendship, and there was a lot occurring during this year. The individual in this dream was looking for relationships that weren't healthy. It was like a disguise. God brought exposure to everything that was secretly happening. There was a lot of intense warfare occurring during this year. Dealing with friendship, sexual interaction, battling mentally, struggling in my sexuality etc.)

DREAM (JULY 12ᵀᴴ)

Me, a friend, and a group of people were walking. We were walking and there was a girl who was calling out to my friend, trying to get his attention. She got his attention and he went back to where she was. Then she kisses him on the lips. Afterwards I called him, asking him why he allowed the girl to kiss him. We were walking on a path to get to school but it didn't look like the school. The way it was set up as if like a game carnival. But him and the girl were flirting with each other. It was like I kept trying to get his attention, but he was focusing more on the girl. (This dream became reality. The friend met a freshman girl in high school, flirting with each other. I tried to explain to him the wrong of what he was doing, being that he was a preacher. Later he regrets it).

At times when we're close to individuals there's a thing called familiarity. They become so familiar with the person that they don't respect the gift. He was so comfortable around me, that the things I foreseen he didn't respect it. So, he rejected what I spoke. Till it manifested, and it wasn't what he thought. You must be very careful with interaction with others. Because respect gets loss when speaking what you see. Everyone will not invest or endorse in your dreams. There's some who just won't have the attention, or intention to listen. Those type of people have the spirit of pharaoh, who heart was hardened and fail to listen to the words of Moses, after speaking what God told him. Pharaoh rejected the words and brought terror on his own people for refusing to listen. Just like Joseph brothers, who refused to see the truth because they were blinded with jealousy. As dreamers, connections can be either detrimental, or beneficial. So, it's very much of importance to watch your surroundings and the people were linked to.

DREAM (OCTOBER 27TH)

I was in this church and there were people who wanted me to go somewhere with them. At first, I was going to go, but I had change my mind. The scenery changes: I seen this gun in front of someone and I pick it up. It was like I was being held hostage, trying to kill me. I wanted to go home. Finally, I escaped, running home. Before I did that, a boy ran ahead of me, escaping. While running there were bullets flying at me, and I got wounded. I finally got close to home. I seen the door crack and enter. Entering, seeing my aunt and my sister. I closed the door behind me, locking all the doors. I was bleeding, while dying slowly. Then, my leader she was in danger, under attack. She was tide up to a fence, being held at gunpoint. She was trying to protect me. But I jumped in front of gun, shielding her. And they started shooting but the bullets went pass us. She protected me, and I protected her. But the whole objective of her being tide up was to keep her out of the way and away from me. In the mix of it all, there was a crowd, watching in broad daylight. So, I untied her. While I was running towards her, to free her, they fire their guns. After freeing her we laid on the ground, while the bullets were flying by they never touched us.

As dreamer, the enemy will attack the people who are connected to you. If he can't reach you, his objective is to destroy you families, friends, community, leaders, kids etc. Protect them with your life. You are a weapon of mass destruction and your opponents will try to kill your future by weakening your existences.

DREAM (OCTOBER 29TH)

I was in this big church. Afterwards, me and my mom were heading to a place. However, I was soaring in the air and I could see demons. And they were trying to stop us. It was

35

as clear as day, seeing them hovering over the earth. We were then on the ground, where we were following people and they were trying to lose us, so that we would be lost. So, we follow them all the way till we reach a place that was familiar. We saw Arda and her car and seeing this big house. Thinking on how when I was in the air, how the demons were trying to detour us, instead I maneuver where they couldn't.

Great call comes with great attacks, a greater warfare, and being pressurized more.

DREAM (NOVEMBER 15TH)

Pastor Latina was speaking what God was telling her to say into the people's life. She called out certain things. In addition, she asks a question, asking do you know who you are? Afterwards, she went to crystal, then my mother; telling my mother to worship God and to do his will. Then she came to me, saying, intercessor. She asks the age of my great grandmother, which was 92. Nevertheless, I hug pastor Latina, crying in worship. Suddenly, different people came up and while they were coming, she was prophesying. She called out someone being adopted. But before that scenery, me and a friend of mine got into an argument and neighbors were watching. We act as if nothing occurred. The scenery changes to him trying to get my sister to preside for him. Again, the scenery changes again, this time I was in a house with Paul, Sierra, and some other individual. I was about to leave to go somewhere and I told Paul that I would be back if it was the lords will. So, me and Sierra went out a door. And I seen pastor cox and Montavius having a conversation. Then she went into the spirit and began praising God. Again, the scenery changes, I seen this elder and she was crying. And she showed me her feet, seeing something growing out of it. She was talking to me while hurting. In the beginning but the ending, there was a big fat man, coming to pastor Latina for prayer. He didn't want to be in the condition he was in anymore. There was a lot of weight on him.

Understanding that there are people who help shape your identity. They have a purpose to help discovery you. Sometimes we become bury with issues and defects that it's hard to find ourselves. But there are individuals who are assigned to identify what is burying the identity and guiding to right path. As well, realizing that there are assignments sent from hell to keep a stagnation. And being that life is fill with people, you must be careful with connections. Connections plays a huge role and have a great impact. Who you hang with that's what you represent. As the saying say, "birds of a feather flock together". Be very observant of your gathering with people. Destiny carry a great sensitivity, it doesn't need the extremes from unnecessary warfare.

YEAR OF 2015

DREAM (APRIL 29TH)

I was going to this class and on my way there I saw snakes in glass containers. A woman was taking them out for people. But there was one container half open, and in it was an orange snake. I open it a little more, and it came out. I ran when it escapes. So, I'm heading to the class and there were more people who came from after. However, I recall seeing a girl in danger. Somehow, I was running from this man, who was looking for the both of us. We hid and played like we were someone else. Entering a room with full of women doing hair. So forth, I went into another room, but it changed. Prior, me and a friend had a discussion and whatever it was, I remember telling him that he was going to keep doing the same thing. Then, the scenery change, I saw water and we had to jump to escape.

DREAM (MAY1ˢᵀ)

There were people that were wearing red and had guns shooting. As well, I had a weapon, shooting at them. And there were two people who came after me and another individual. I ran and jumped on top of a vehicle. But they were persistent. They didn't stop. So, they chase me in a church. We kept fighting. I saw water, planning to overthrow the individual within. It was like a war going on between good and bad.

DREAM (MAY 11ᵀᴴ)

I was in this place and it was a lot of people. And I was looking down a dark hallway. I seen a child and a car with sharp objects sticking from it, trying to kill him. In defense, I blew in his direction, causing it to miss him. I went down there and seen a person trying to escape from a woman, but they died. I ran to the front where the others were. A friend of mine was going down the hallway and I warned him not to go. Instead, he went anyway. Then, a man privacy got cut off. Me, or someone else hollering warning the people. We all ran. I got the keys and a boy breaking through the glass and we ran out. I jump in the truck about to drive off. Then I woke up.

YEAR OF 2016

As a dreamer you experience many emotions. Sometimes frustration, anger, rejection etc. As I said in the beginning, dreams are not always about others, or foreseeing the future; but it shows you, you. Identifying different areas, like an open procedure. Undergoing procedures takes many precautions and instructions. Then, the real surgery happens with dealing with the real issues; which leads to cutting and handling what is detrimental to the body. There are people there for the delivery and healing process.

DREAM (OCTOBER 24TH)

I was in class full of different people. We were taking a draft. After we got done, we graded each other papers. Suddenly, there was a fire alarm going off. It wasn't a drill, but it was real. So, the teacher postpones the test to another day. Everybody ran outside of the building. But I ran home.

In life we're face with different trials and test. We are put in situations to build character. Some test are drafts, or either called pre-test. Meaning that it takes training and practice and upbuilding of character in preparation for what is much greater. Life evolves every day, not knowing what will occur next. This dream seems not so profound, but it's the little things we should pay attention to. Even the little things have great impact. But we undergo test after the test seeing where were weak and what needs improvement. Noticed, in the dream due to the sounding of the alarm and seeing that it was a practice, but it was real how everyone panic. This shows how they weren't prepared for the bigger test, the real drill. Many times, we put on a front as if we are ready, and prepared. But it takes being equip, fully armored for what's up ahead. So, worrying doesn't help, panicking doesn't help, becoming frustrated with the process doesn't help etc. We must understand the preparation of what's building stamina, character, and strength. Just because you failed the first time or the other times, learn from your mistake, your error, your failures etc.

DREAM (OCTOBER 22ND)

Me, Latoya Wiggins, and Minister Wiggins were in the truck driving on this hill. While going uphill we seen water puddles. It was a great amount of water puddles. The water was at the top of road, about to come down. But before we did we turn around, making a detour. On the other hand, I remember being at a church. My pastor told Montavius to pray and that I needed prayer. However, before he prayed, he got prayer for himself. As a result, there was deliverance, which led to him purging. They got the paper towel. He yelled, saying, that there were three of them. But the woman that was praying for him, touch his head. After he was done he begin to pray for others. He prayed for these marry apostles, by the name of Gibbs. So, prophet Redmond prayed for me and she started prophesying. Saying, "prophet…." I started hollering, giving God glory. Eventually, Montavius prayed for Latoya Wiggins which cause her to be laid out on the floor. He touched her stomach, which caused her to purge. The scenery changes: this dude was in this store and a person ask him was he gay and he admitted it.

Being called comes with issues. Its as simple as it is, you have struggles, but it does not identify who you are. There are people there to help you overcome and step out of your puddle of blood. People with true attentions, motives will help you birth and reach your true potential. One way to deliverance is admitting. Admitting doesn't make you weak, but its makes you vulnerable to getting free and delivered.

It seems at times where those who were close to me, I could foresee death and it would occurred. There were certain people that was dear to me, before they exited this world I seen it. An example, my leader, by the name of Patricia Cox. She died in the year of 2016, in the month of April. But prior to that month, she had appreciation service and that very night I dreamed we were in a church service and the spirit of God was strong. A pastor began to prophesy, saying, "when you leader goes up so shall you men." Afterwards she left, and in the back seat of the car, something occurred with her heart, which cause her to die. And I cried, wondering who will take over from here. I awoke, late that night and I text her, seeing was she awake. The ironic thing, is that she was. Later that morning, I finally told her what I seen. But simply, she told me she wasn't going anywhere, having work to do. The next month, she announces to the church that had to take a rest that she didn't want to take but she had to. Before she died, I visit her in the hospital. One morning I get a phone calling telling me she was gone, and I cried. The church took a major blow from her death. But the good that came out of it is we became better, we took what she taught us and grew with it. Some elevated to a higher place, and some went back out into the world. This is proof.

I will say her legacy didn't die but lived to carry her investment. But she wasn't the only death I foreseen. Even those deaths caused me to weep.

DREAM

I was speaking to this lady and she didn't speak back. But when my friend spoke, she was responsive. I became angry with him and I wanted to fight him. Afterwards, the scenery changed. There was a prophet who was getting delivered but had a demon that got cast out. And she came to me and asks was it out.

Afterwards, the next day our church had an event for my Pastor. This woman and her daughter came inside the event. Her daughter spoke but she didn't speak. Then I noticed she spoke to a friend of mine instead and I felt some way. I was angry, and I didn't say anything to him. As a result, this proves and shows how what you see can birth reality. In the book of Genesis, the forty chapter. It sums up how Joseph was imprisoned, and while in prison there were two men, a cupbearer and baker; who had dreams and needed an interpreter. Being that Joseph carry the gift of interpretation, he was able to interpret their dreams. Long story short, after the interpretation the baker was attack by the very things he seen, and the cupbearer was restored back to his rightful position. So, it takes depth of studying. Symbolism are unique and sometimes hard to understand. However, there are moments that God speak through symbolism to get a message across. I reminded of Daniel the second chapter, explains how a King name Nebuchadnezzar's dreamed of a kingdom inferior to his will dominate his kingdom and overtake it. There were words use like iron statue, iron ceramic, gold, bronze etc. Another example, Abraham Lincoln, who was the sixteenth president. But before he died he dreamed about his death. Three days before his death Lincoln dreamed of wandering in the White House searching for the source of mournful sounds; he kept wandering until he arrived at the East Room, finding a corpse covered, guarded by soldiers and surrounded by a crowd of mourners. Lincoln asked one of the soldiers who died, the soldiers replied, "The president. He was killed by an assassin." Soon after he died in the way he seen it.

DREAM

I was in a fire and I had to get out and I did. While in the mix I begin to see a man pulling people out of the fire; but as I was getting out the pole lines was laying down. As I was escaping I was getting scratch. Also, in the mix I saw three white chairs and one of those chairs were for me. There was a relative of mine who had a baby and she got into a conflict with another person. But the most terrible that happen to her was her baby being taken. Understand to every suffering there's a process called reign. In preparation of the reign, there's a before process we must go through and it's called suffering. Suffering has a way in producing and shaping a king, and a product of golden. Purifying the impurities, which birth a new individual. While facing opposition there's doors opening, table prepared, and seat at the kings table.

Dreams come with deep meanings and deeper revelation.

DREAM

I saw people on this bus going to a certain location and they were being held hostage. first time around this person was attempting to escape but got wounded. so, it was like a replay, it just kept repeating. After successfully escaping, they ran into a fence becoming stuck. Nevertheless, they were persistent to getting on the other side. Therefore, they plan to find an escape. Ironically, I find a hole to escape. Successfully making it on the other side a woman was on the other side of the gate. She looks as if she was Islamic or Muslim; dressing with a black scarf wrapped around her face and head, white shirt and black dress. She was saying something. Finally, we escape, seeing different cars. I sat there and begin to think on what happen within. Thinking on how the enemy or the very situation were in will hold us captive.

And the adversary doesn't want to see freedom. By way of failure always try again. Never give up. The enemy job is to make it hard on you. His main objective is to kill, steal, and destroy. So, understand the disguise he uses to acquaint with people to get their heart. Even to become familiar with weakness, secrets, understanding the mind. However, if the adversary can break the mind, he'll become control of the body. It then becomes a vessel that he occupies for his use. If he can create a blockage then he'll create a clogged. Where there's no source of flow. Train yourself how to dismantle, disarmed, sterilize etc. the opponent schemes. You are a weapon of mass destruction. You're also the key the future, you have what the world need and that's a dreamer. Having the heart of a dreamer can become a weakness; loving people, sharing dreams, giving access to the insight. Allowing the entry to be open, you have now given trust way to whom you thought love you. But really, they despise your gift to see, your very existence, the gift of prophecy. Your foresight is important to destiny and the future. Don't allow the dream killers, or the destiny blockers get in the way. Furthermore, no matter who they are understand what it takes to protecting what is sensitive and pure. You are the one that can change the nation, and the people around you. Are you the Joseph within turmoil? Will you still see when they try to take your sight (dream)? Don't allow rejection or being unwanted to keep the dreamer in you restricted. Understand that what's in you can birth a legacy's. In my years of living I've faced many obstacles. From the time of conception, till the time of maturity I've struggle to understand my identity. Trying to understand what was in me and how to grow in it. There were moments I ran from destiny, denying, and fighting against what is meant to happen. I fought against rejection, dealing with molestation, sexual immortality, rage (quick temper) etc. Experiencing the pain and the cost of being who I am. Before ever discovering, there's always layers of scars, and then there's a pathway call journey. As a dreamer you're capable in seeing the near future. That is what you face the hardest things in life, and you war so hard with destiny because you carry the gift of prophecy. There's a future attach to your sight.

Overtime, I grew spiritually, learning from my mistakes, my failures and my errors. I had many downfalls. There were battles that should have killed destiny. But in my spiritual growth, my insight and foresight became sharper and deeper in dreams.

In the year of 2017….

DREAM (DECEMBER 14TH)

I was laying in this place. I believe it was water as first. As I laid there, and focused things began to change. It was like stars everywhere. But it was a very beautiful water and great sight to see. Then a great figure of God or the angel he was big, gigantic. I became nervous. As I was under he showed me a spring. But he touches me and there was a refresh, nothing like this touch. It was different very different. I remembered him picking me up and he sat me in his lap, honestly. Then he started talking to me and I remember eating something. It was junk food and he told me he doesn't want me eating it anymore. After I came from under I started telling my cousin. I was telling them get in and see. One fell and went in this hole. Eventually, the water lit up again, but they were afraid to get in.

Transitioning into a new year, understanding that this next level flesh wouldn't be able to enter. It takes changing of appetite (not only in the natural but spiritual). After seeing this dream, I realize that some people will not be ready to enter a great realm. Because they either don't believe or their afraid. This dream scared me so, causing me to feel nervous. Because I saw angelic being. He was huge, and it was like no other. I could feel the very sensation of when he touched me. I turn my head and seen that he was so close to me. Entering the deep requires dying to self, crucifying the flesh part of who you are. Imagine stepping into realms as great as this. You'll be so amaze of where you go in the dream world. If the enemy can cause insomnia, by keeping you from dreaming, then he'll try limiting you from seeing.

In the year of 2018.......

DREAM (APRIL 9ᵀᴴ)

My aunt drove into what looked like empty trailers, but outside of the trailers look like junk cars. We went inside. But inside were different doors. Also, there were people there, but they weren't of human kind. They were demonic and very much soulish. We were trying to get away, trying to keep us hostage. There was a doorway and hell were behind it, only the dead live there. Me and the others were trying to escape from demons that were behind us. We were rushing to reach the top of the stairs, getting away from them. I recall even one of the individuals weren't human neither one of us, but they were trying to escape too. The demons didn't stop. So, it was something that need to be done. The portal (doorway) of hell need to be close. So, the demon had the key to shutting the door. In my hands the door could be closed. Eventually we were able to leave. Me and pastor Kendrick had to do something. We had to open the heavens. So, we came back and there was a lady who was showing us what needed to be done. But beside her a demon came and it was in the form of a girl name crystal. After opening the heavens, we ran. But the demon was trying to pull me with it.

The greater the launch, you'll enter dimensions that goes beyond the earth dimension. Always stay in posture. Know your surroundings. Learn how to handle hostile atmospheres. There's so much hostility roaming the earth, don't conform to this world. Be you and unique! There's more to come. YOU ARE THE FUTURE!!

Printed in the United States
By Bookmasters